THE DUNES
ART AND PROSE

SUSAN HYNDMAN

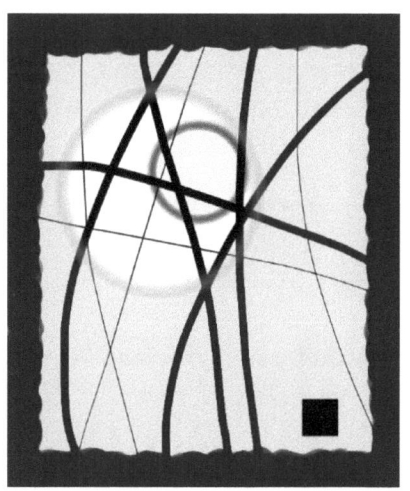

CONTENT PAGE

WEAVING .... 8 - 9

CORN HUSK .... 10 - 11

SPIN OFF .... 12 - 13

MONET GARDEN .... 14 - 15

TRIANGLE LOVE .... 16 - 17

ROCKY SHORE .... 18 - 19

UNTITLED 1 .... 20 - 21

ROSA VERBENA .... 22 - 23

UNTITLED 2 .... 24 - 25

CUPCAKE .... 26 - 27

LILY PONDS .... 28 - 29

A LOOK INSIDE .... 30 - 31

ACROBAT .... 32 - 33

SIGNAL NORTH .... 34 - 35

VIVIENNE .... 36 - 37

CACTI 1 .... 38 - 39

SUBURB .... 40 - 41

LEATHER PETAL .... 42 - 43

MAC HOUSE .... 44 - 45

WEST .... 46 - 47

SANCTUARY .... 48 - 49

"WEAVING"

Threads on a loom woven to capture
intangible shapes of the mountains.
Spruce, hawk, antelope and creek
wander throughout.

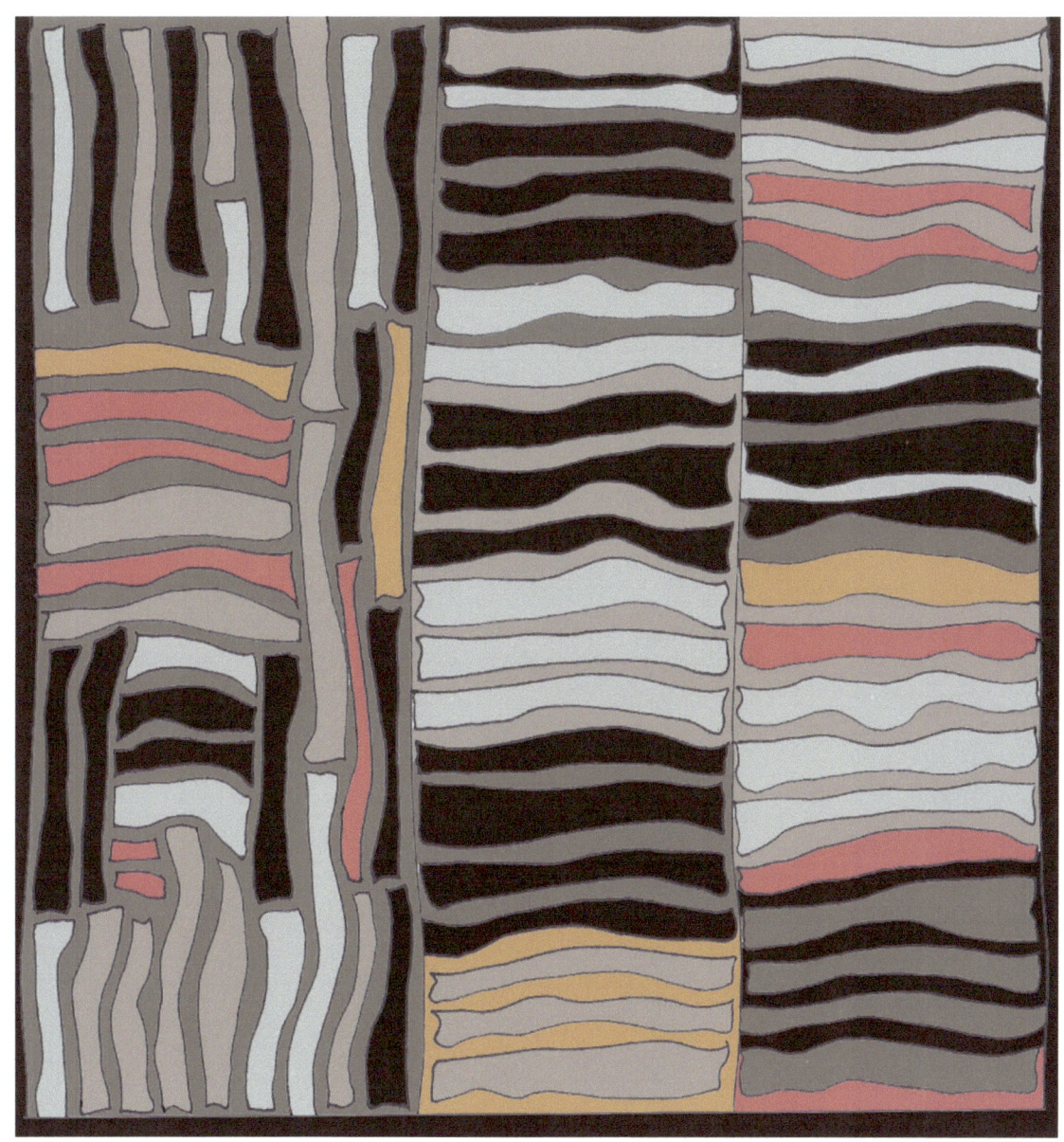

"CORN HUSK"

The combine threshes madly, ripping through miles of pale, sandy fawn, collecting layers of fabric like the dawn. Beige kernels rustle and expand my memories of winter.

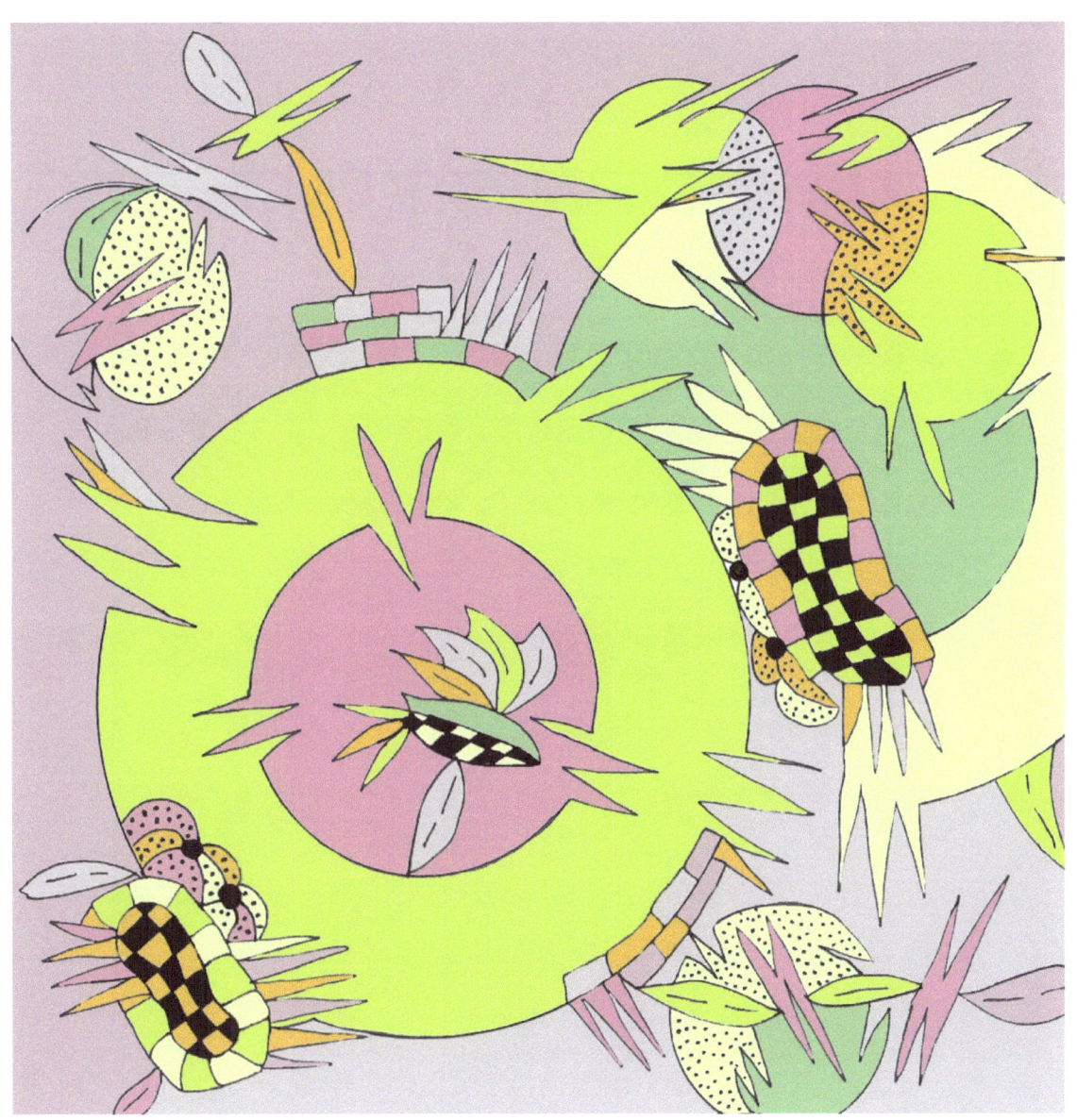

"SPIN-OFF"

Reminiscent of a puzzle, or a set of
mutant checkers on a backdrop of sand. I
envision the circles floating above me in
space like a mobile. I embrace the
simplicity of being young again.

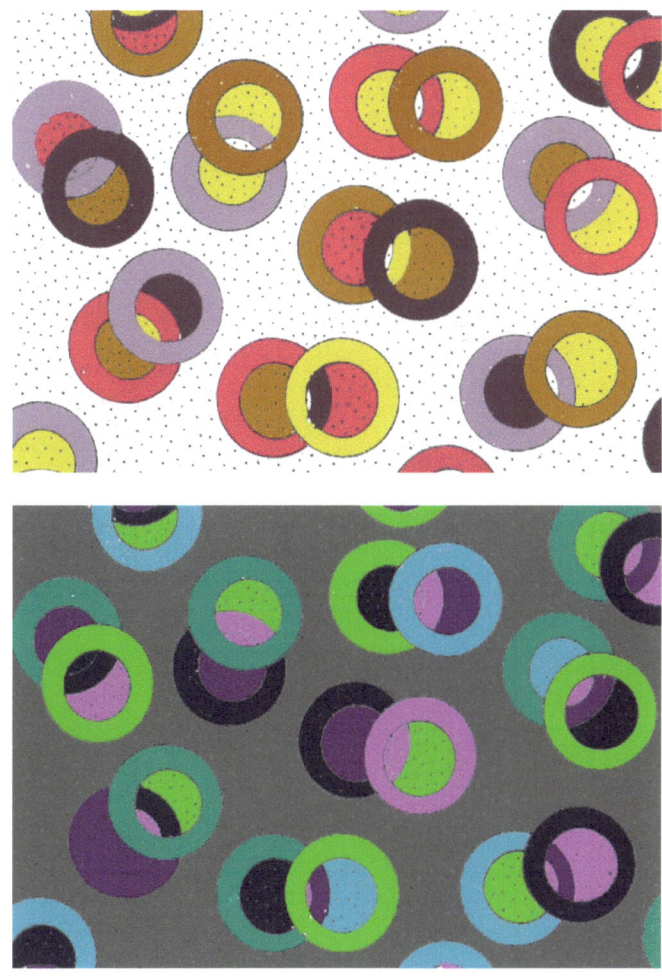

"MONET GARDEN"

Enchanting water lilies of Monet's
Giverny. Magical, timeless and spiritual.
Walk with me through the meadows that
open to every dream you have ever had.
Each time I look upon you I am mesmerized.

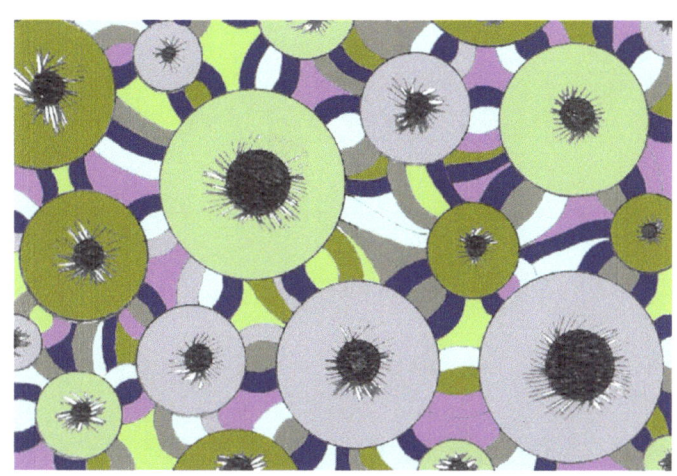

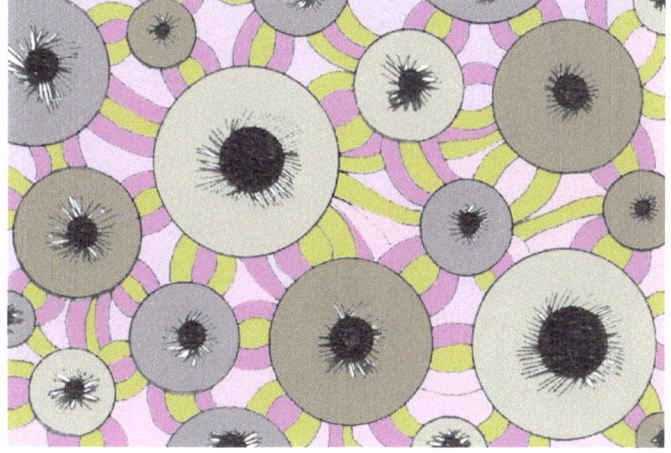

"TRIANGLE LOVE"

IN A MOMENT THE RAINBOW SHONE BRIGHTLY AT THE HORIZON'S EDGE. A MILLION ABSTRACT WAVES CRASHING TOGETHER IN AN OCEAN OF HUES.

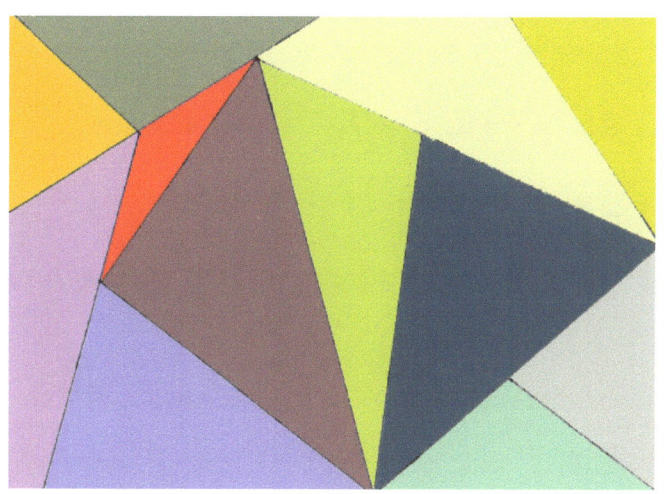

"ROCKY SHORE"

FRAGMENTS OF ROCK AND CLIFF SIDE WRAPPING UP WITH THE TIDES. A SHORELINE JUST AHEAD, JUTTING OUT TOWARD THE SUNRISE.

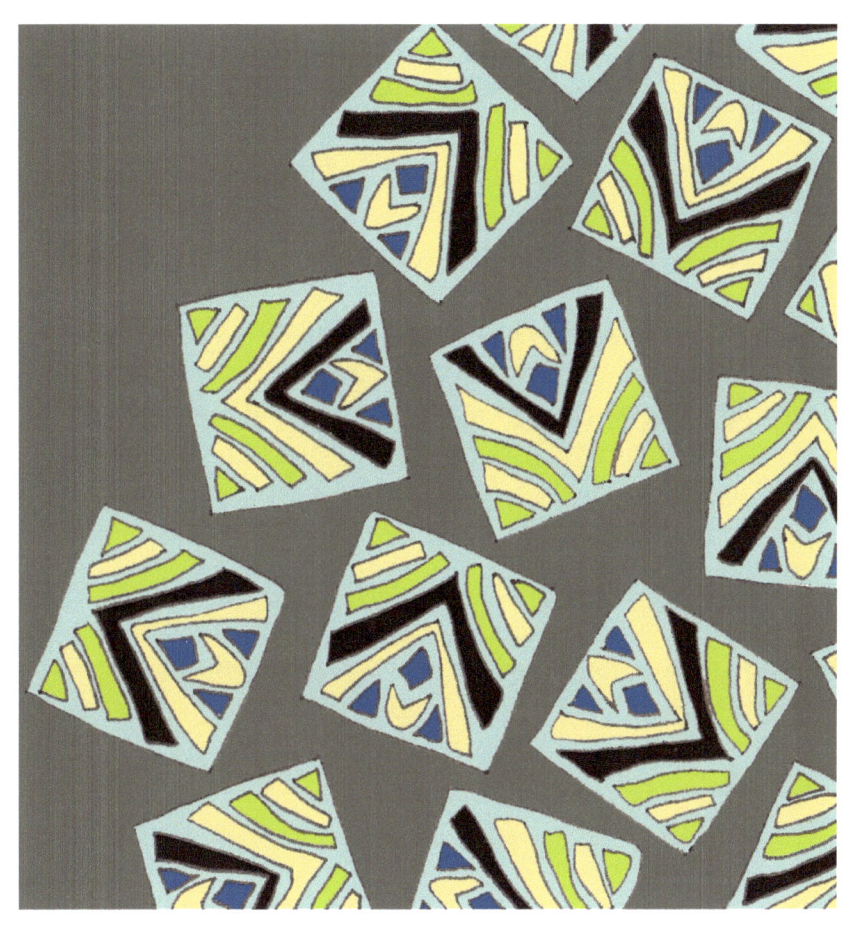

"UNTITLED 1"

A pair of kaleidoscope glasses peering out over a rim of coffee. The stranger sips quietly at an outdoor Italian café. He is suddenly startled by a flock of birds.

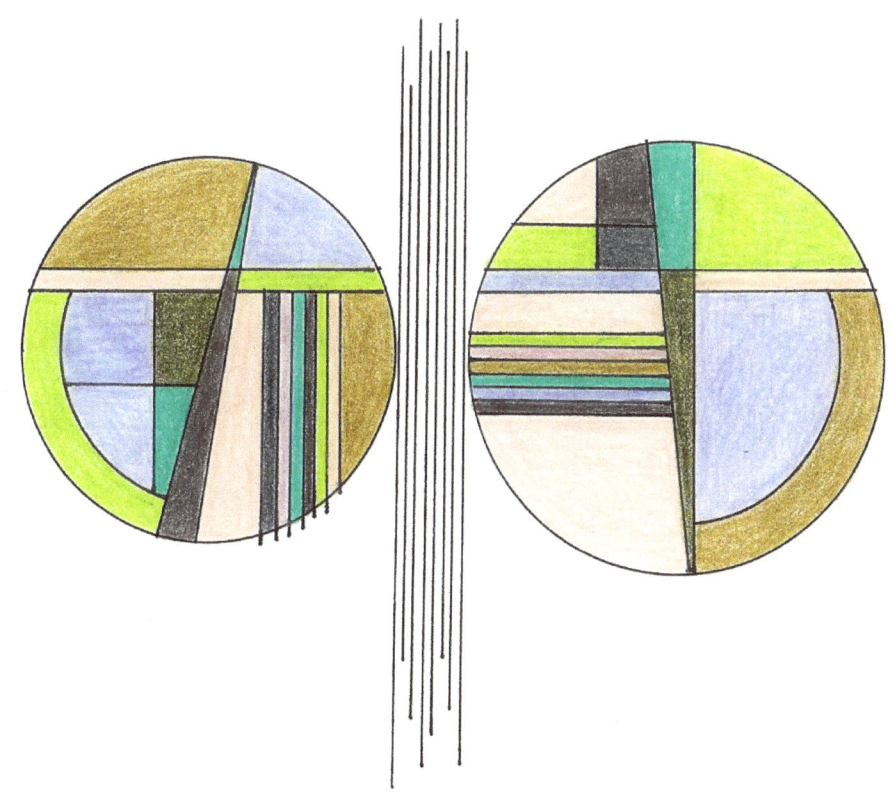

"ROSA VERBENA"

She draws a singular breath and descends the stairs, gliding toward the flashes of light, unlimited in her potential. She takes the air out of the room. Silence. Drawn from memories of a backyard rose garden.

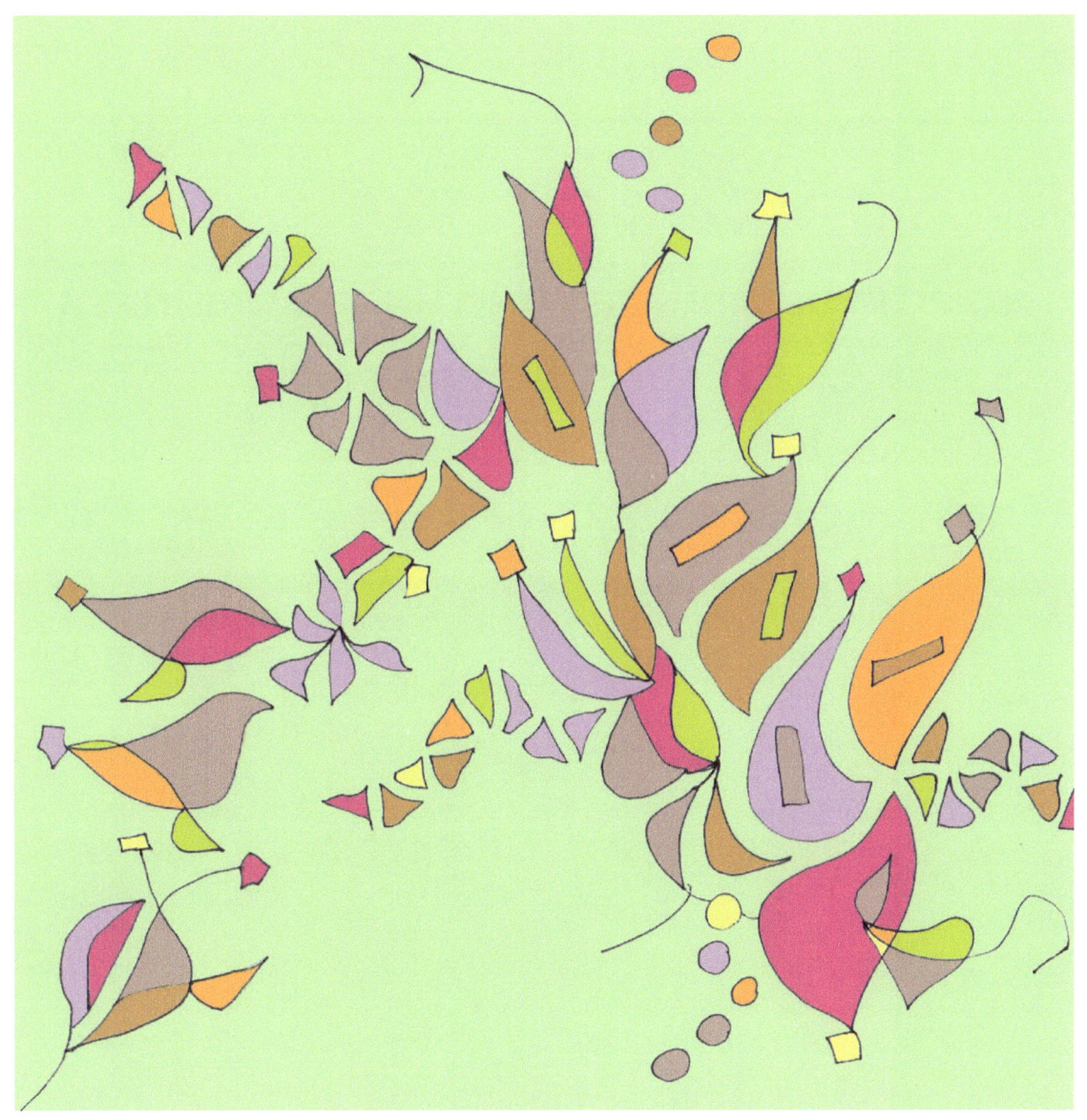

"UNTITLED 2"

The flow of water rustling through many mouths of pipe, resting under cabinets and landing at my feet.

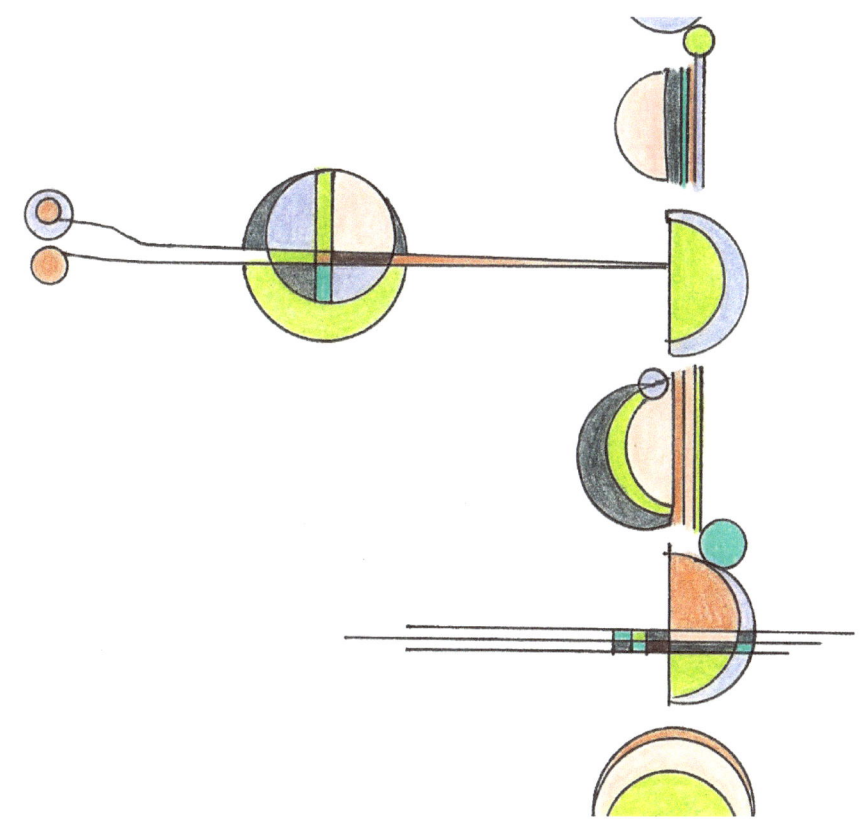

"CUPCAKE"

Tier by tier, a building emerges adhering to the draftsman's precise architectural renderings. Many levels of stairs and places to hide.

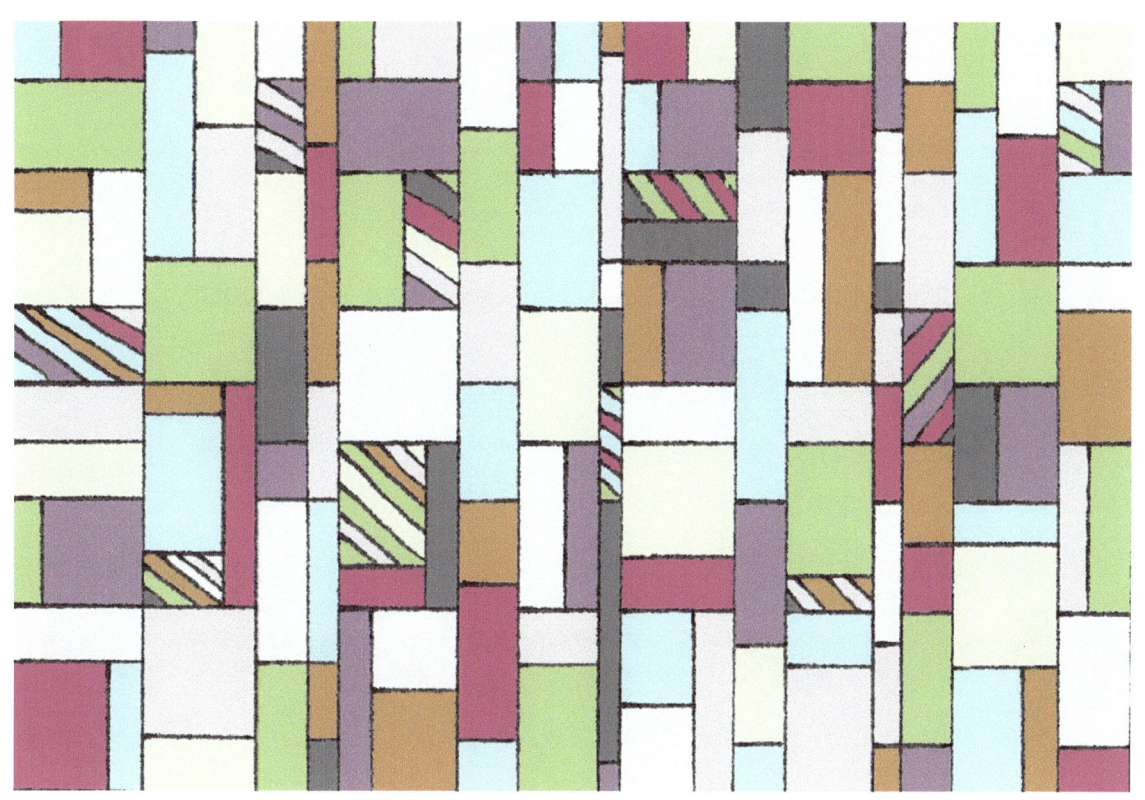

"LILY PONDS"

In the wilderness, far from the familiar the traveler reaches down to inspect a blossom drenched in sunlight and morning dew. It comforts him.

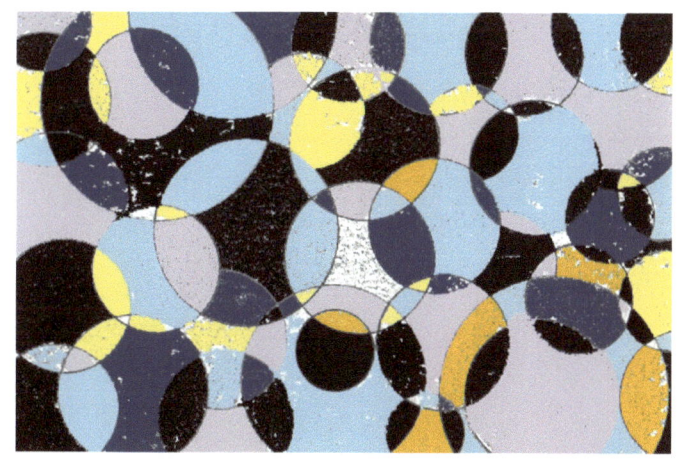

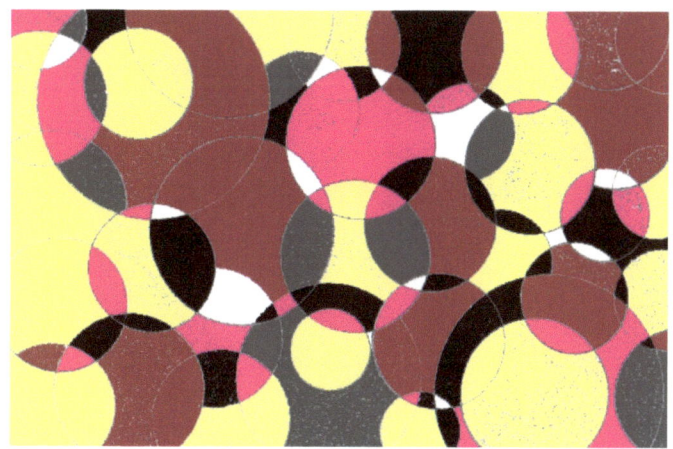

"A LOOK INSIDE"

WHEN I DROP THE COINS INTO THE FOUNTAIN
AND MAKE A WISH, THE GLITTERY METALS FILL
THE BOTTOM AND MIX WITH ALGAE AND LOVE.

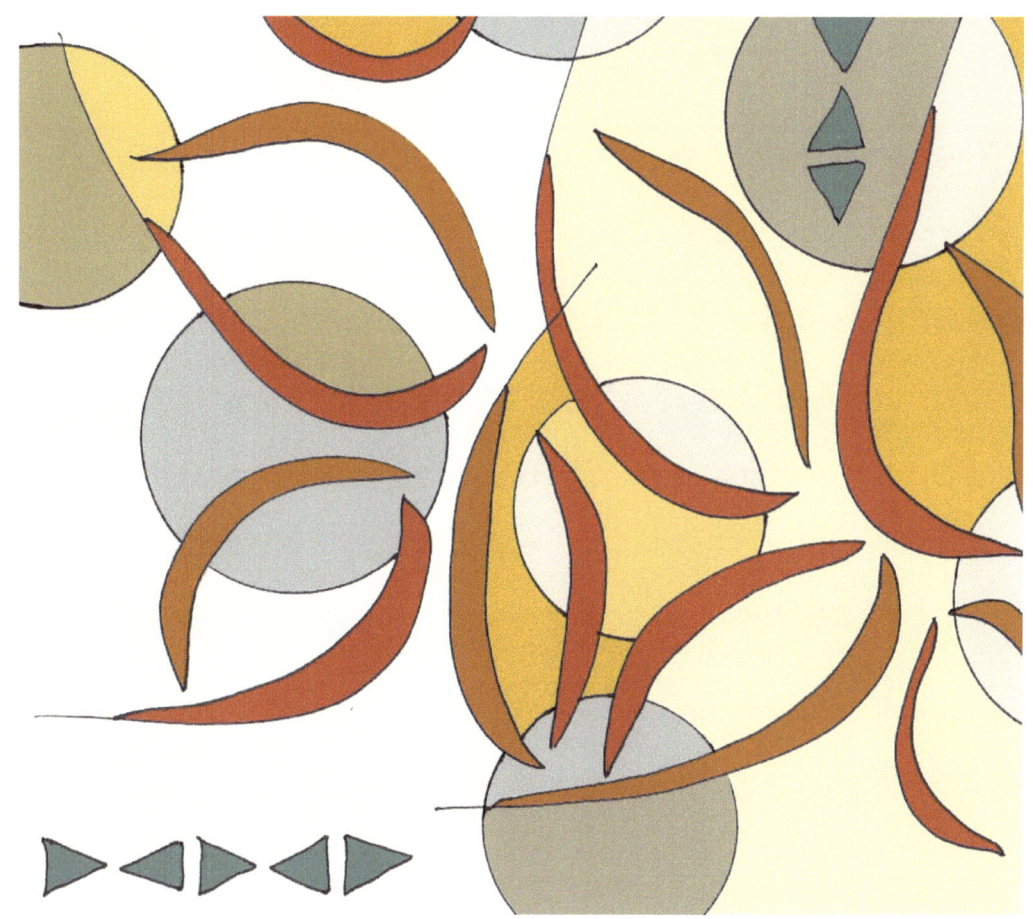

"ACROBAT"

THE DAREDEVIL RISES ABOVE CLOUDS OF
PUTTY, WHISKING CALLOUSED FEET ACROSS THE
NARROW WIRE WITH NO SAFE LANDING PLACE.
IN A HEARTBEAT, HE TRAVERSES MILES OF
WHITE TO REACH PARADISE.

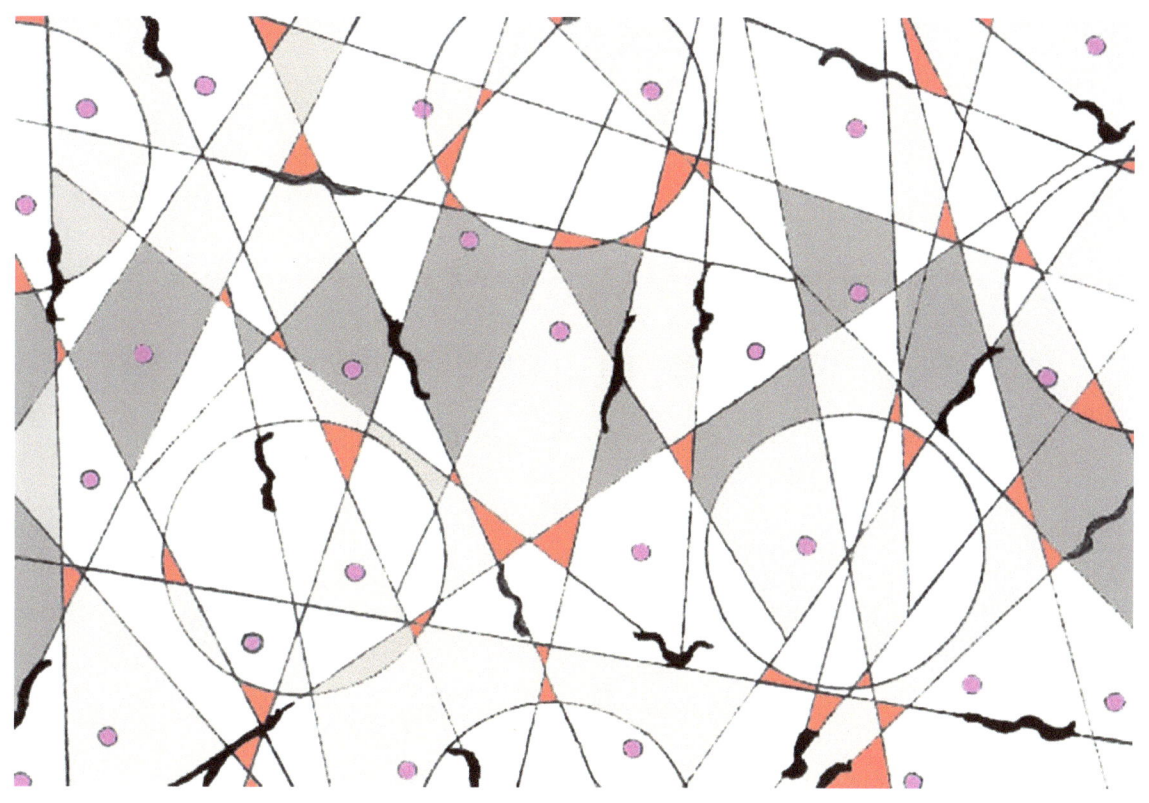

"SIGNAL NORTH"

Mr. Jungle cat ascends the rooftop stealthily and waves a Mardi gras mask. In the spring he is joining a traveling circus to operate the Ferris wheel.

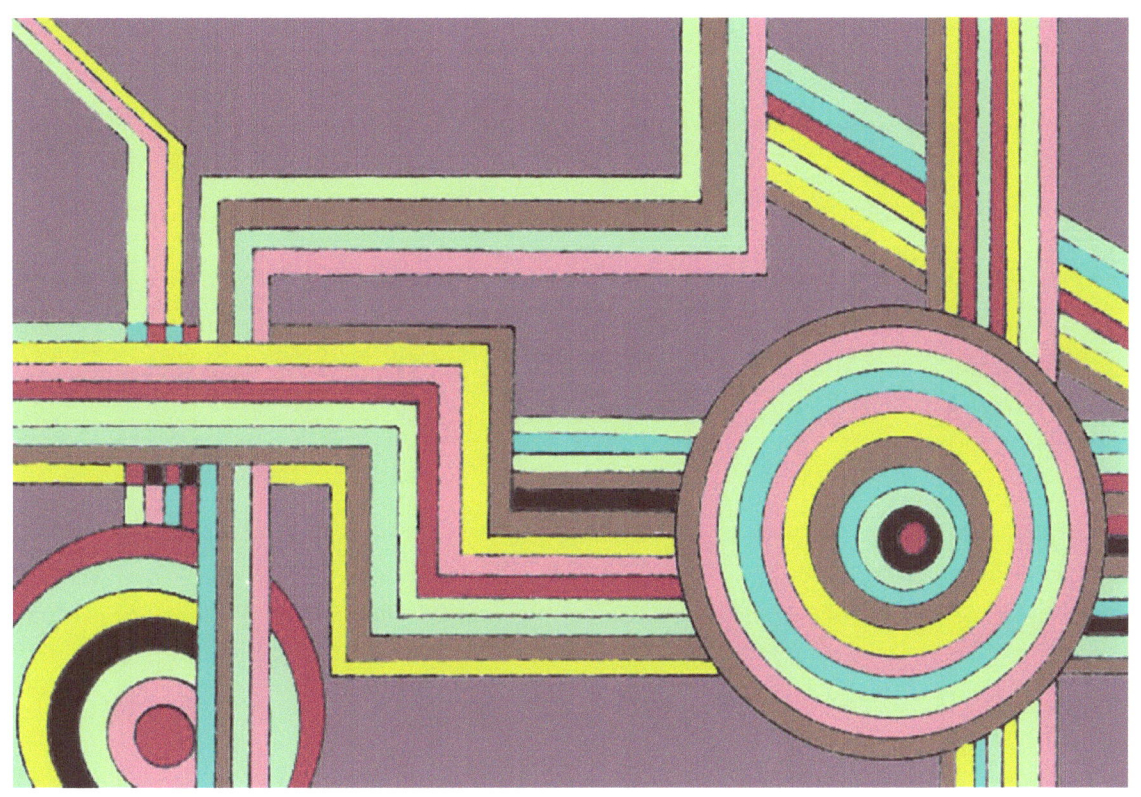

"VIVIENNE"

Fine blades of grass zig zag the plains in the Camaro's rear view mirror. Explain to me the pageantry of sunrise in my imagination.

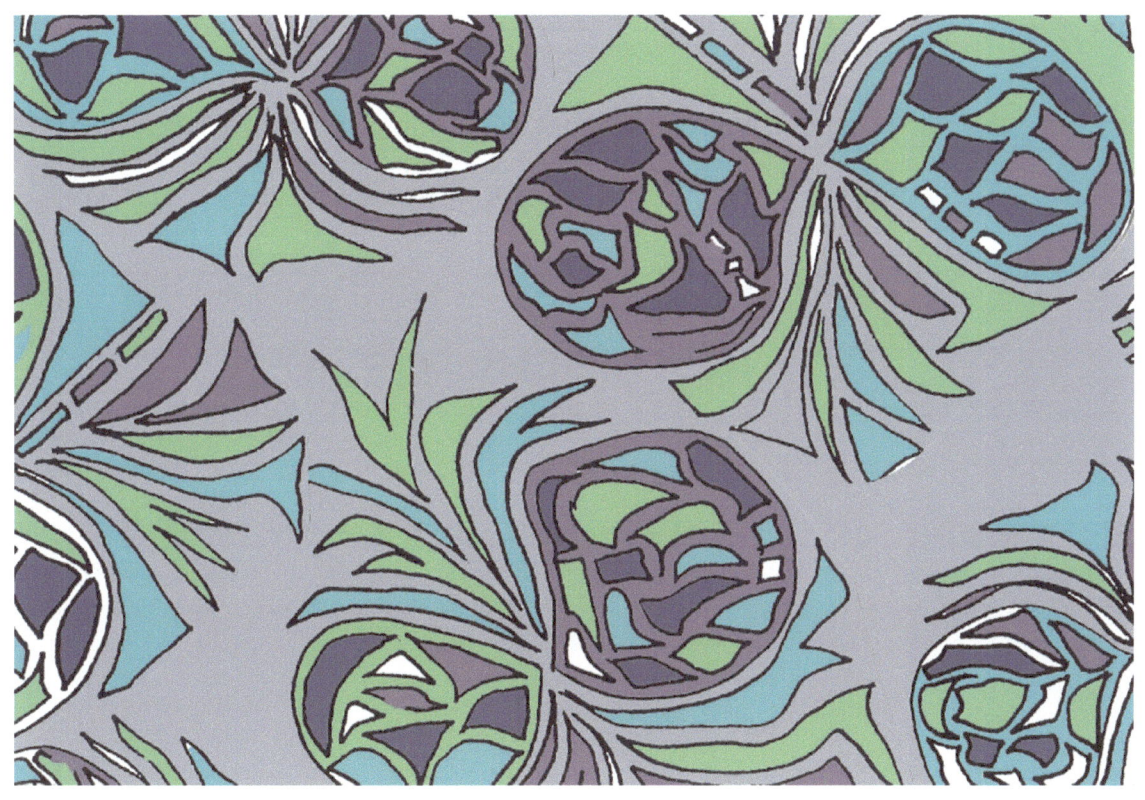

"CACTI 1"

THE LITHE AND ELEGANT SWAN WEARS ANGORA AND COWBOY BOOTS IN HER DEBUT AS QUEEN ZOLA IN THE SCHOOL PLAY.

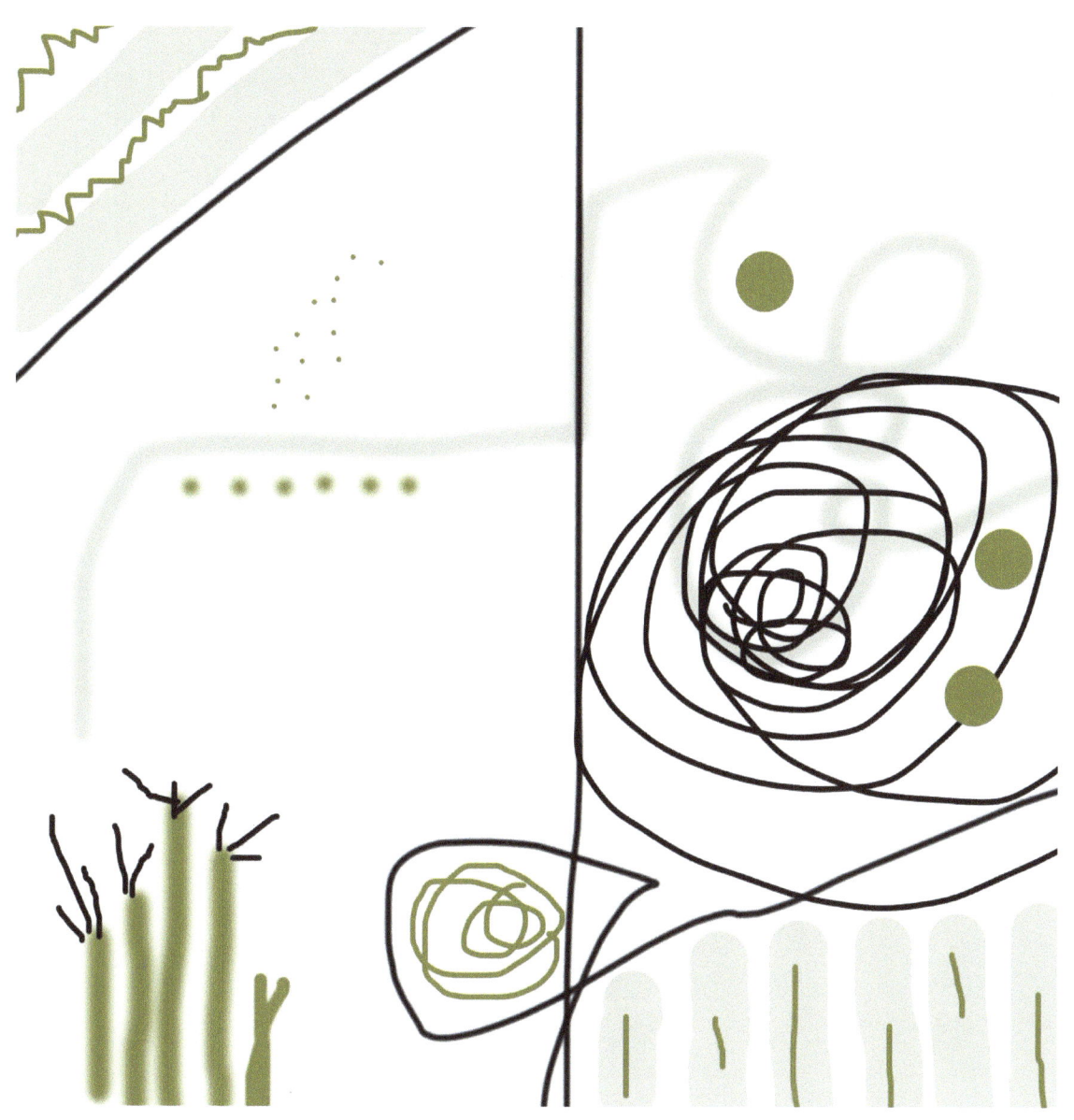

"SUBURB"

The dog has no agenda. She laps up water from my soul. The ball she chases carries all of my emotions. Scrambled, they weep out onto the floor.

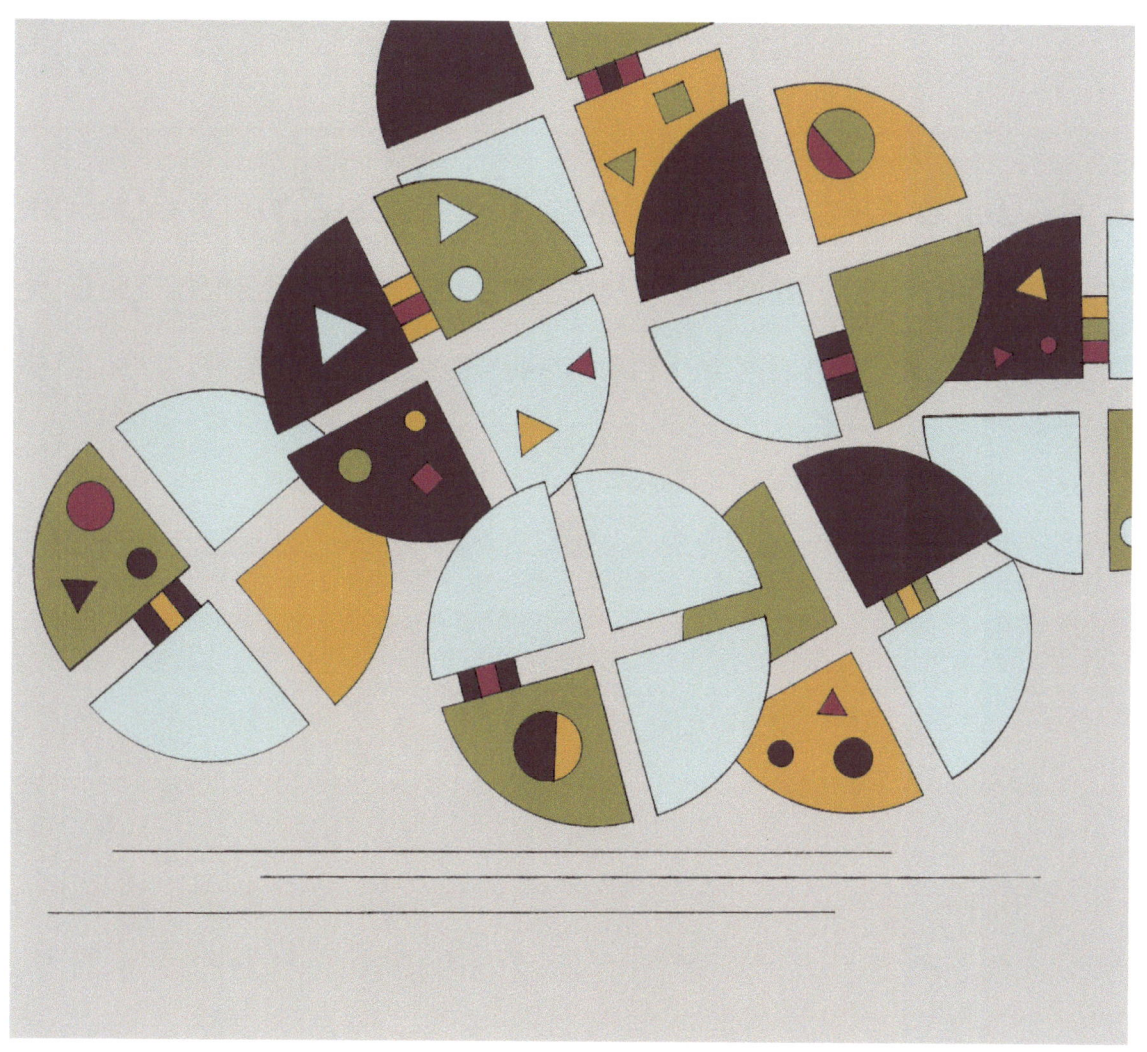

"LEATHER PETAL"

DRAINED FROM WASHING THE BLUE TINT OUT OF HER HAIR, BEULAH REGRETS SAMPLING THE BROWNIE WITH WHIPPED CREAM.

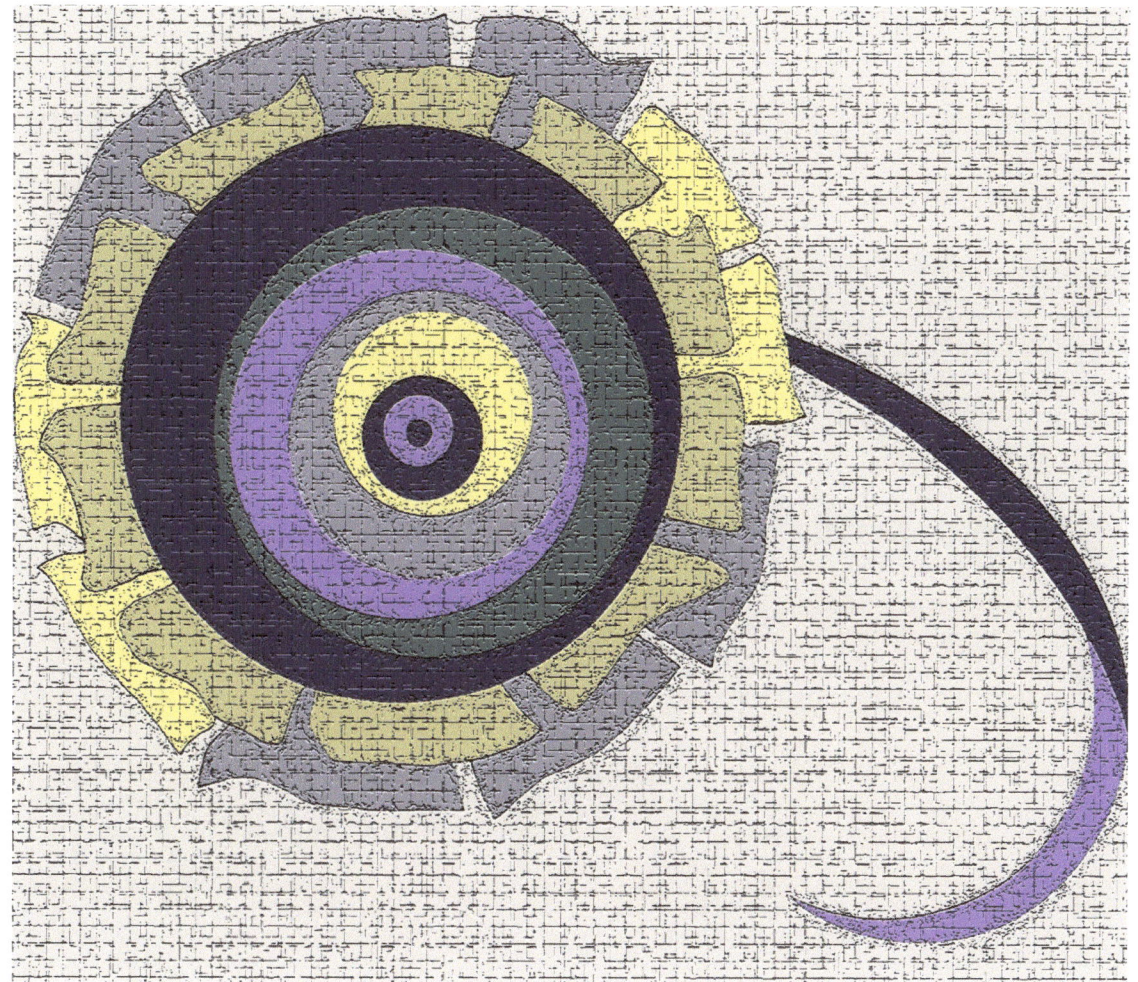

"MAC HOUSE"

A cry rang out in the night from the East.
I bury my head in buckwheat and await the
dawn; Spanish moss seeping onto the bed.

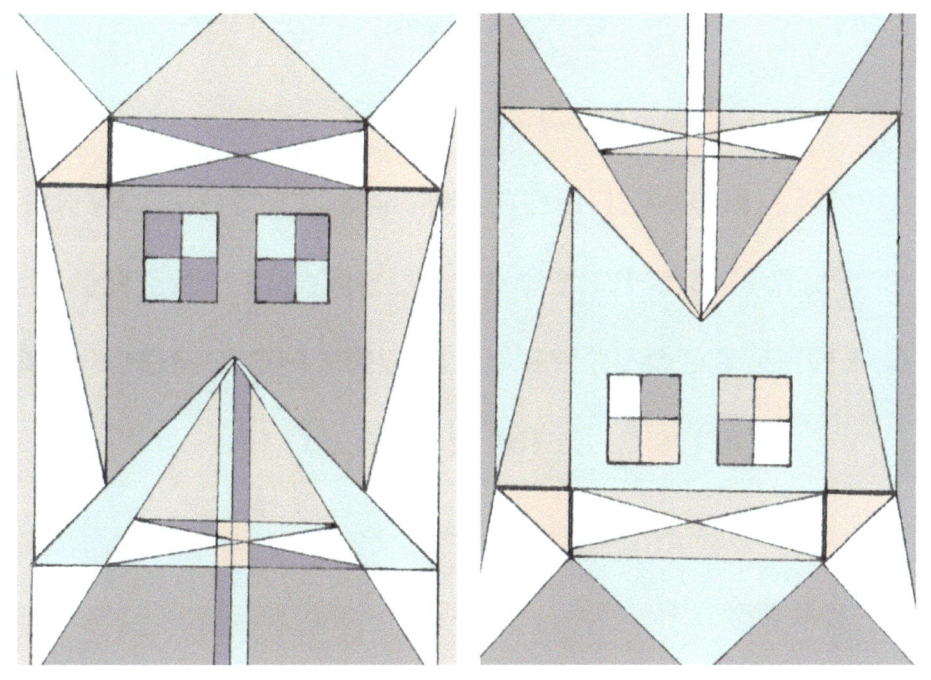

"WEST"

A sacred knowledge of mint chips warms the bowl of candied twigs. With zero toil, the blanket covers all of the chocolate stuffed in my mouth.

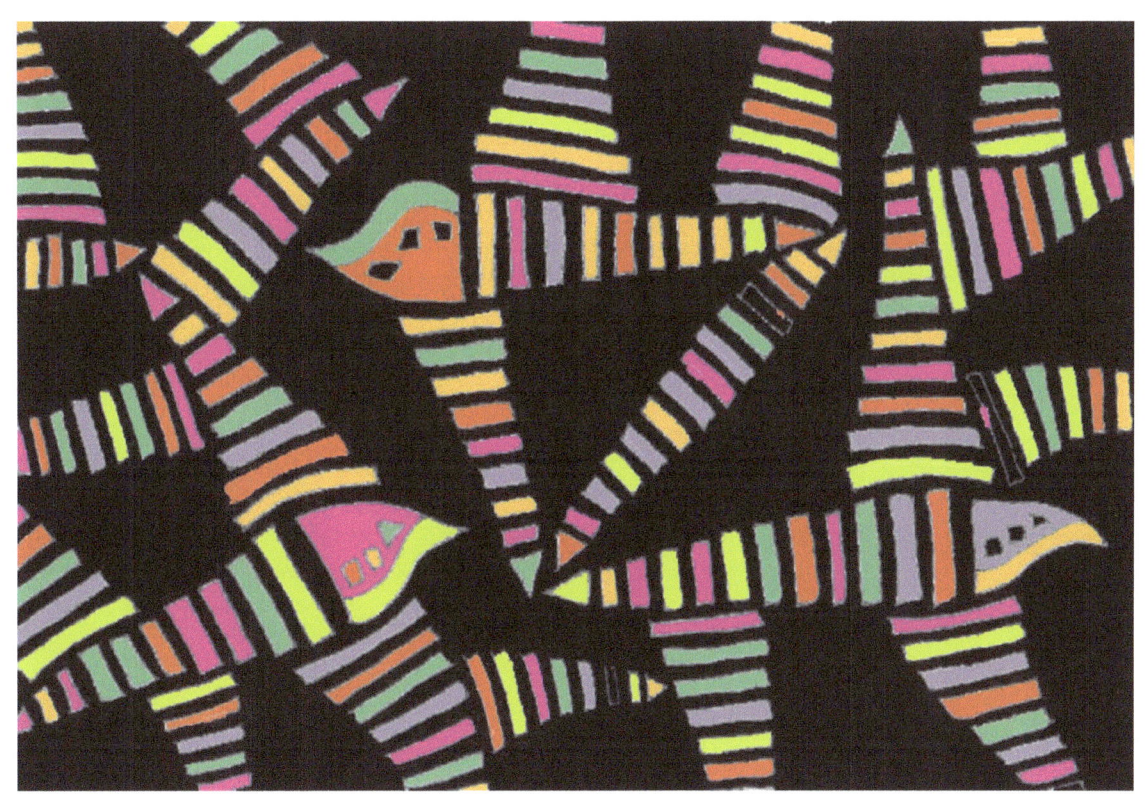

"SANCTUARY"

The taxi arrived quietly. Each suitcase brimming with treasures from the moon. I spy a lime green and saffron ribbon curling over the monkey's tail.

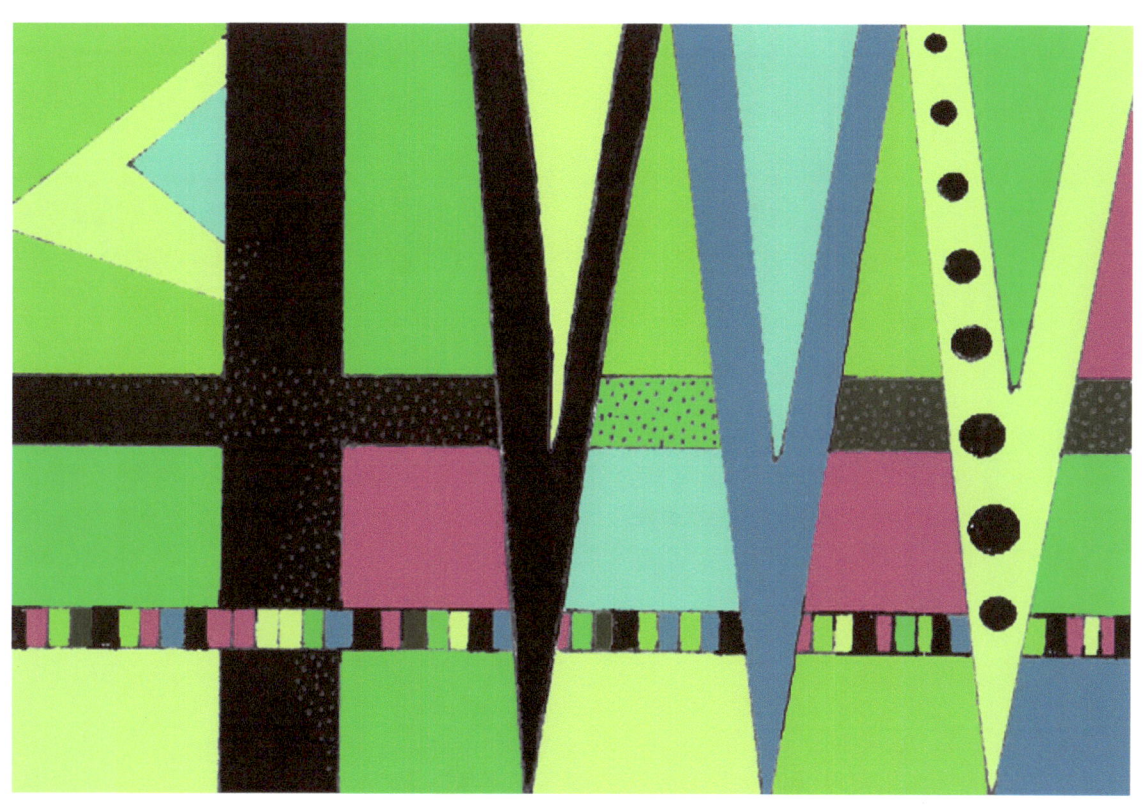

A Sand dune in shadow dwarfed by the cobalt lake lurches toward violet and lemon May blossoms........

SH. 2014

www.ingramcontent.com/pod-product-compliance
Lightning Source LLC
Chambersburg PA
CBHW050818180526
45159CB00004B/1713